FATOU
PURSUIT

***

Shawnee Green-Tucker, Author
Eric Naymor, Illustrator
Ileta E. Randall, Layout Editor

***
***

A Fairy Tale
"Forgiveness is the key to harmony and peace."

Copyright © 2012 Shawnee Green-Tucker
Printed in USA by Greater Is He Publishing, LLC

All rights reserved. No part of this book may be reproduced or transmitted in any form or by any means without written permission from the author.

ISBN 978-0-9852800-1-7

Greater is He Publishing
9824 E. Washington St, Chagrin Falls Ohio 44023
P O. Box 46115 Bedford Ohio, 44146

http://www.greaterishepublishing.com

If you would like to book this author for story time at your school, please contact Greater Is He Publishing at (216) 288-9315

Acknowledgement

I would like to dedicate this book to my cousin C.C. Morrison who allowed me to view his writings of the Lion and the Leopard from which a line of his work prompted me to create this fairytale of Fatou. I would also like to thank my cousin for giving me the name of his sponsored child in Africa, when I was looking for a little girl's name, which turned out to be the main character in this book.

Also, I would like to thank my cousin for supporting me through this book's developmental stages (typing many of my ideas onto paper that gave my ideas life). I would like to thank my cousin for his suggestions even though, many times, we did not agree but he endured the storm. And most of all, K (cousin), I appreciate you for your desire to improve society through your hard work writing "The Lion and the Leopard," and wanting to see the writings become a reality of being our brother's keeper.

It was that thinking (from your writings, and the sentence you unselfishly allowed me to use), that pioneered the way for "Fatou and the Great Pursuit". K, your intellect and advice will not go in vain and someday you will reap the benefits of your labor.

Cuz'n

Introduction

Long, long ago, there was a great Hunter who was chief of many villages. He and the villagers lived in peace and harmony. One day, an evil Warrior came against the Hunter and his peaceful villages, to make war.

The Warrior took over the villages and his evil grew great upon the land and for many years and generations to come, the land was filled with the unquenchable evil of the Warrior's spirit but a little girl filled with love and hope ...

A bus driver was sitting on a chartered bus, nervous and in a state of shock. The driver had a look of unbelief on his face as he continuously shook his head back and forth. "Oh no!" shouted a little boy who had stepped onto the bus. To the little boy's surprise, it was apparent the bus driver was very upset. Someone had just robbed him as he sat waiting for the neighborhood children at a designated bus stop.

The driver jumped out of his seat and started pacing the bus up and down, back and forth …"What am I going to do? What am I going to do? I've just been robbed! I can't take this anymore! I just can't do this!"

Every Thanksgiving Day, SuperMart would sponsor a charter bus to take the neighborhood children to the zoo. This was how the mega department store could show their appreciation for the community's financial support of their business.

The trip was an annual event that had begun 35 years ago, by SuperMart, and was highly anticipated among the neighborhood children; and now, the unfortunate incident had caused the trip to be cancelled indefinitely. A police officer came to document the report, still shaking, the bus driver returned back to work but vowed never to return back to that neighborhood again.

The bus driver approached Mr. Applewood, his boss, "I am not going back to that neighborhood as long as it remains dangerous". Hearing the news and feeling the need to protect his employee, Mr. Applewood went to the neighborhood to talk with the residents. He explained, "For many of you, the Thanksgiving trip has been celebrated over several generations. Given that, I know that this will be a lost and a big disappointment, but Mr. Jayrel, the driver, will not be returning to this neighborhood. He refuses to make any more annual trips to the zoo… now and forever. He is very fearful and refuses to return, so this bus trip is cancelled for good! I would never want another driver to experience the trauma of fear that Mr. Jayrel felt. And I definitely don't want to take a chance with children boarding the bus, let it be forbidden, if this would have happened when children were boarding, I would never forgive myself! I will not allow my driver to continue, knowing the dangerous situation in this neighborhood and knowing it could turn for the worst."

Mr. Applewood sadly walked away from the children shaking his head and feeling remorse because he had to remove the long standing and loyal partnership between his bus company and SuperMart; and most of all, he regretted leaving the children disappointed and hurt. But no longer could he allow his driver to be placed in harms-way while picking the children up for their annual trip to the zoo.

Once they heard the disappointing news, the children were very unhappy, but nevertheless, they were still worried about Mr. Jayrel, the bus driver. They loved him so much, and the children all knew just how much he loved them. However, hearing the bad news, a young girl named Fatou became very upset with Mr. Jayrel for not returning but deep down inside she knew he was right. Her neighborhood was no longer safe as it was when her parents first moved in. Through Fatou's disappointment, she told herself, "That's it! I am going to find a way to make my neighborhood safe again." She thought, "No longer will the residents of this neighborhood live in fear."

Fatou believed that everyone, whether in her neighborhood or in another neighborhood, should not have to live in fear. That is not what a neighborhood should represent. She thought about her neighborhood and what her parents and grandparents said it was like when they were young. This motivated Fatou into thinking of ways to make her neighborhood safe.

Fatou began to remember that her grandparents once gave her a Manuel entitled, *The Good Neighbor.* Fatou started to think about the lessons in the book which she had read. The lessons explained what a good neighbor was and how to become one. Fatou also recalled what her grandparents and parents told her about becoming a good neighbor and knowing how important it is when living with others in peace and harmony. She recalled their words, "It is a divine desire for people to live together in love." Fatou realized how selfish she was acting by only thinking of herself and what she wanted for herself, the trip to the zoo. She then thought of Mr. Jayrel and how he could have lost his life trying to make others happy.

As Fatou pondered her thoughts, she realized just how awful it would have been if Mr. Jayrel's family would no longer have him around to love and treasure the way she loved and treasured her family. Fatou also started to reminisce about the times her neighborhood was filled with beautiful butterflies and happy bright fireflies, which have since left because of the ugly despair and violence that has now filled her neighborhood. There was no more beauty that filled Fatou's neighborhood, and now, the trip to the zoo was being discontinued. While Fatou thought about the possible outcome of the trip, she became humbled and convinced her friends to follow her. Fatou informed all the children of the neighborhood that she wanted to hold a community meeting. Then Fatou said, "I think I have an idea that would bring Mr. Jayrel back and once more make our neighborhood a safe place to live and visit."

Inside of Fatou's heart, all she wanted was to once more have a neighborhood that everyone could be proud of, and not feel ashamed to mention where they lived. Fatou then pulled out her copy of the Manuel, *The Good Neighbor*. She started reading, "The good neighbor is a good and very positive title to have. The good neighbor is one that is trustworthy, honest, and mature. It means to be a positive communicator, show respect for humanity, watch out for each other, help each other when and where there is a need, and very importantly, a good neighbor is friendly and courteous."

While Fatou was reading, her friends listened very attentively. On their way home, the children discussed what they learned from Fatou's book and could not wait to tell every child in the neighborhood what they had learned at the meeting. When Fatou stepped outside the next morning, a large crowd of people from the neighborhood had filled her front yard. Many of the neighbors that filled Fatou's yard, that day, were children, but many adults were present too. The adults and children were wearing garments that represented the culture and heritage of their ancestors, long ago. Fatou looked upon the garments as a symbol of unity and pride. Seeing this, Fatou knew the meeting was important to her neighbors. She also knew, as tears fell from her eyes, just how important and needed her meeting was.

Fatou's grandfather picked her up and stood her on top of a wooden box. As she looked out over the large crowd, Fatou spoke with pride of her neighborhood. She described it through the innocence of a child's eyes. She did not see all the ugliness of the violence that was now present in her once beautiful neighborhood, instead, Fatou saw her neighborhood as it once was, and how it will be again. Fatou spoke about her neighborhood with passion, "I see houses on my street. To me they aren't just houses, but castles filled with kings, queens, princes, and princesses. They are our relatives and friends. Yes, yours and mine! They are our families. We are all connected. And that means we are brothers and sisters! We are one unit!"

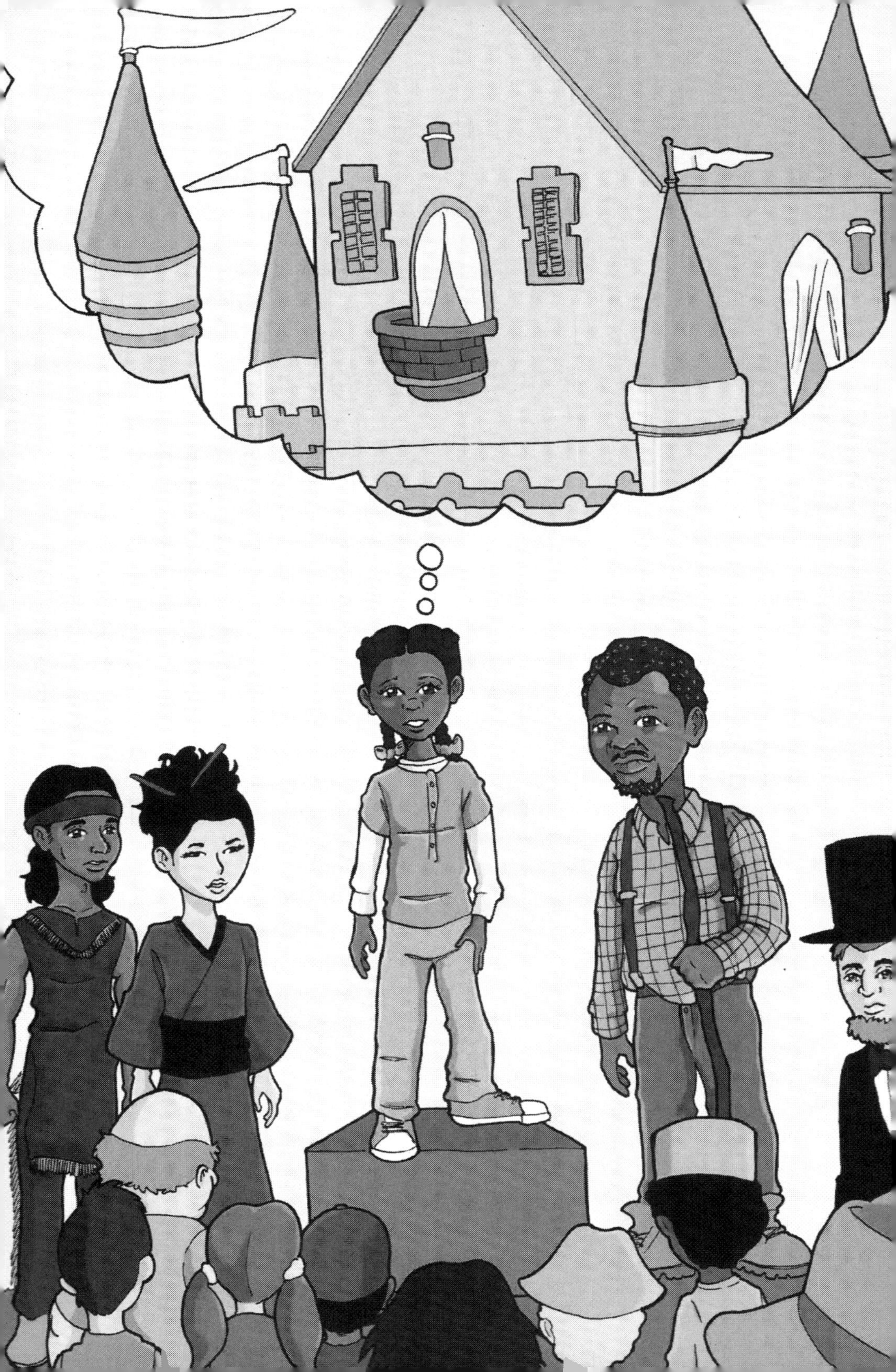

After Fatou spoke, the crowd was inspired. They all knew it was time to unite and take back their community for the generations to come. The adults were amazed to hear a young girl speak with such wisdom and strength. For once, their hope was kindled toward the youth of today. The adults were convinced once they heard Fatou speak, that a young child leading the way would make for a stronger tomorrow. And the adults realized that everyone has something to contribute to society whether young or old. And everyone agreed that it was time to put away their petty differences and work harder to live together in love, peace, and harmony. After the meeting, Fatou's grandfather appeared concerned but at the same time, excited. Grandfather shouted with excitement, "Fatou! I need to borrow your book bag! Everyone, quickly, give me whatever you have and put it in Fatou's backpack." Grandfather began to make his rounds within the crowd. He went from neighbor to neighbor asking them to put their things into Fatou's backpack, things such as their family heirlooms, from their cultural ancestors.

Grandfather referred to the neighbors' items as family treasures. He thought, "I have to get these precious treasures to the mountaintop." After Grandfather left the neighborhood meeting, he went back home and sat down in his favorite chair. Grandfather began to think about the ancient graveyard and of all the ancestors that lay, unattended, on top of a mountaintop several miles away. As he thought, Grandfather decided to pay a visit to the ancient graveyard the next day. Fatou's grandfather rose early the next morning. He reminisced about all the things he heard his granddaughter speak to the crowd about, and how she wanted to come up with a way to bring Mr. Jayrel back to the neighborhood, and restore the annual trips back to the zoo. Grandfather remembered a folk tale which his father had told him about a Hunter and a Warrior.

He thought to himself, "The Hunter was a great king and leader of many villages." He also thought how his father told him about the villagers, and how they believed in living with all people in love, peace, and harmony. However, there was an evil Warrior who did not believe in the Hunter's way of peace. The Warrior did not like the Hunter's positive values and principles, instead, the Warrior believed in taking what you wanted by force. And because of the Warrior's negative spirit and attitude, there was much anger, hatred, and violence that spread among mankind and throughout the ancient land." In fact, the old folk tale told of the many lives and villages that were destroyed at the hands of the Warrior, and how his evil spirit continued to spread throughout the earth, even today.

The folk tale continues, as Grandfather remembered that many of the villagers were believed to have been buried in the graves, along with the Hunter, in the graveyard on top of the mountain, just outside the city. As Grandfather decided to make his travel to the mountaintop, one of the neighbors, who had been at the meeting, drove him midway to the mountaintop and let him out of the car. Grandfather had to walk the rest of the way to the top because it was too dangerous for a car to safely travel to the top of the mountain.

When Grandfather reached the top of the mountain, he looked around with sadness at what his eyes saw. The graveyard did not resemble a graveyard, at all, but instead, it looked more like an abandoned field that had not been attended to in many years. He saw the graveyard had been trashed, and that no real love and respect for the ancestors' graveyard had been shown. Grandfather realized the times had changed and the respect and honor for those that went before the generations had diminished. With heartfelt emotions Grandfather thought, "It doesn't look like much, it has no fancy headstones or markers. It was just a plain field on top of the mountain."

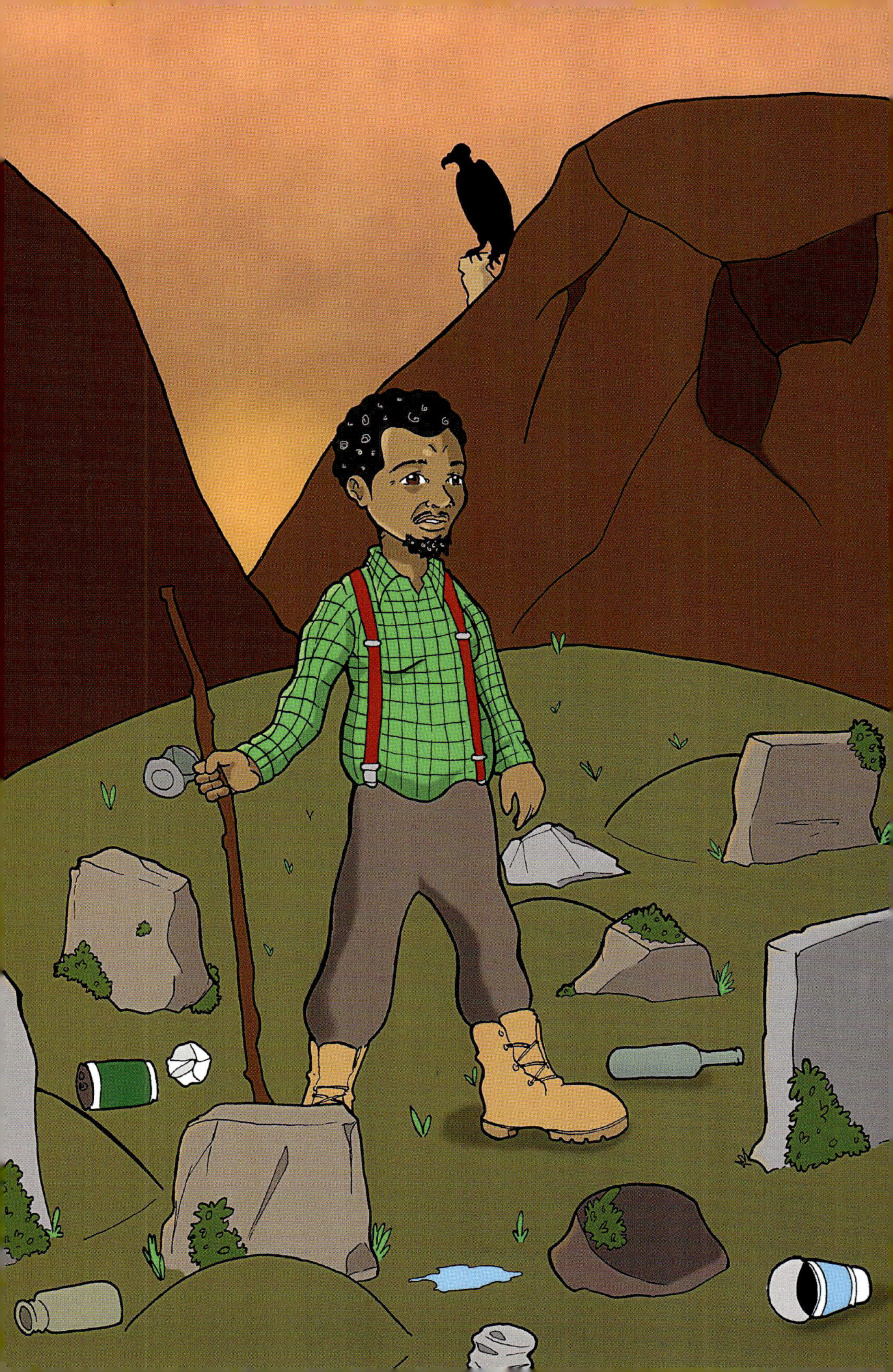

Grandfather thought just like his neighborhood, the ancient graveyard was just as special, and equally important. As Grandfather entered the old burial site, he asked his ancestors for permission to visit upon their sacred ground. He humbly spoke, "Oh! Ancient One of the past, I humbly submit myself to your great powers. Please do not be angry with my presence, but see my presence as giving honor to your place of rest, and grant me your permission to enter." Grandfather then stepped inside the sacred burial ground and pulled the neighbors' family treasures from Fatou's book bag. He held them up toward the sky as he shouted, "Great One! I offer these jewels to you as family treasures. Please except these gifts as tokens of honor to you from all your decedents, here on this Earth." Grandfather asked for the ancestors to help bring the bus driver back and restore love, peace, and harmony back to their neighborhood.

When the time had come for Grandfather to go back down the mountain he knew he was alone, but somehow, Grandfather felt like a friend had come to join him on his way down the mountain. As he walked down the mountain, Grandfather felt a strong wind blowing around his feet, but just as it came, it suddenly left. Grandfather's journey to the burial grounds had made him weak and tired, but the sudden wind that blew refreshed him. He knew the wind was good and could have been an omen, or sign, that something good was going to happen. Grandfather got into his neighbor's car and went back to town. He never once mentioned the strong wind he felt leaving the graveyard.

The sun was setting and a tired hometown traveling salesman stopped his car at the bottom of the mountain where the ancient burial ground rested. Every year the salesman would come home for Thanksgiving and assist with the children's trip to the zoo; but before he would reach his hometown, to settle in for the night, he would always stop to pay his respects at the ancestors' burial site. The traveler was ready to retire for the night (after his long ride home) but before he could, he parked his car at the bottom of the mountain and walked the rest of the way to the mountaintop. As he came near the top, the traveler thought that he was dreaming. He could see an ancient African village forming over the mountaintop. The salesman rubbed his eyes thinking the village would go away but the village was still there. The image was forming and appeared over the ancient graves. In shock, the salesman shouted, "Holy smoke! I really need to get some rest." So the traveler decided to go back to his car to rest he thought to visit the graveyard in the morning because it was getting dark. The salesman tried to get some rest in his car, but he did not sleep much because he heard voices of excitement all through the night.

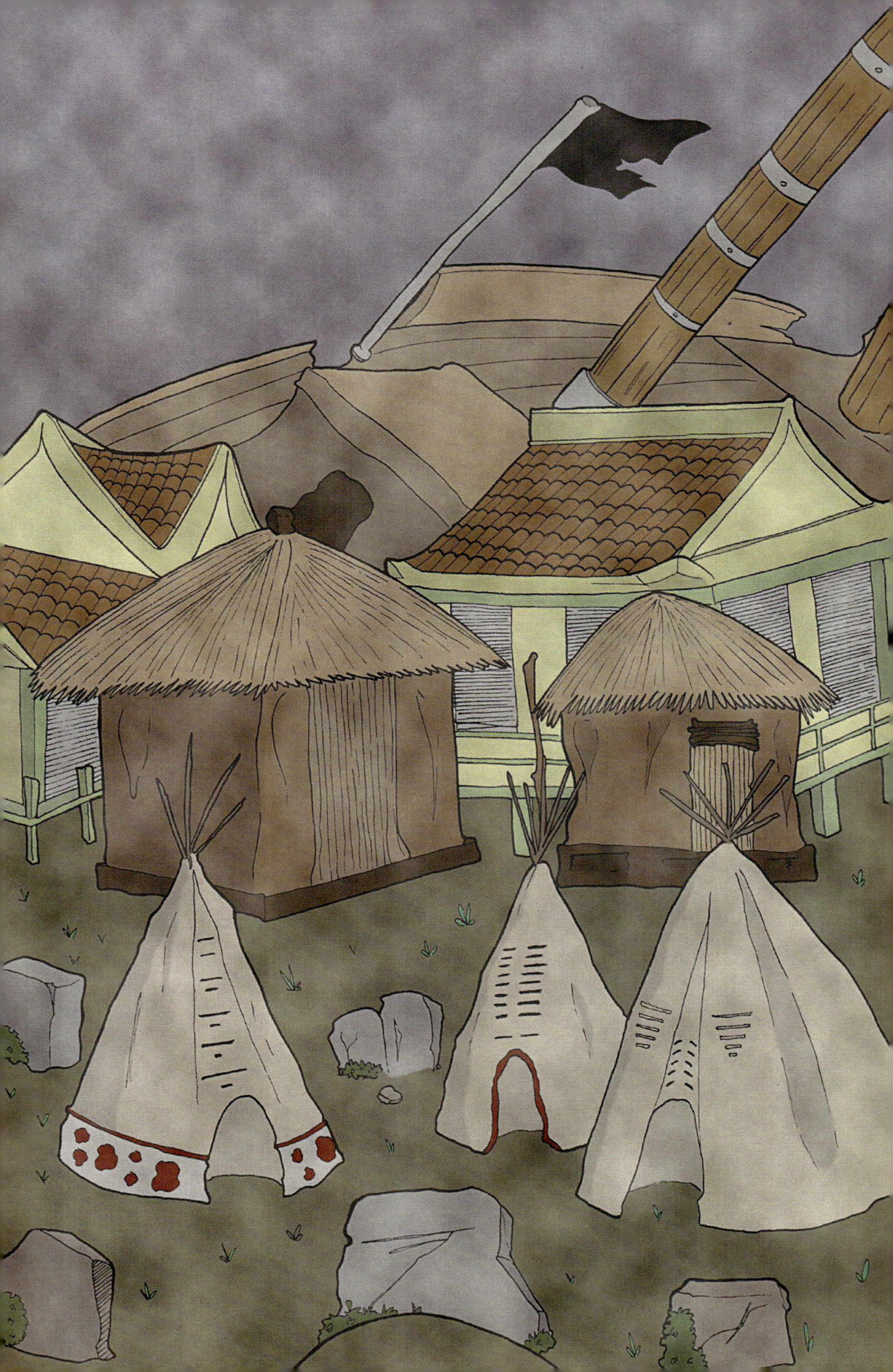

By the middle of the night, many villages of other cultures had appeared on the mountaintop, and the Hunter was standing in the midst of them. Grandfather had awakened the Hunter's spirit with his presence. The wind that Grandfather felt was that of the Hunter shaking out his cape before putting it on. The Hunter went from grave to grave waking the spirits of old, the men of the old villages that were once destroyed by the Warrior long age.

The Hunter was anxious to give the news of Grandfather's visit. The Ancient Ones came from many cultures such as African, Asian, European, and Hispanic. The Ancient Ones of the village respectfully spoke to the Hunter with their weary voices. They asked, "Why do you wake us? We were so comfortable. Is the news that you bring so important that you wake us from our long rest?" The Hunter replied to the men, "Our descendents need us. We must go to the city. Many of our great-great-great-grandchildren are in trouble. They make war upon one another in armies they now call gangs. The villages that they live in are also called neighborhoods which are not safe for their very existence. Some of our descendants are doing well but others are not.

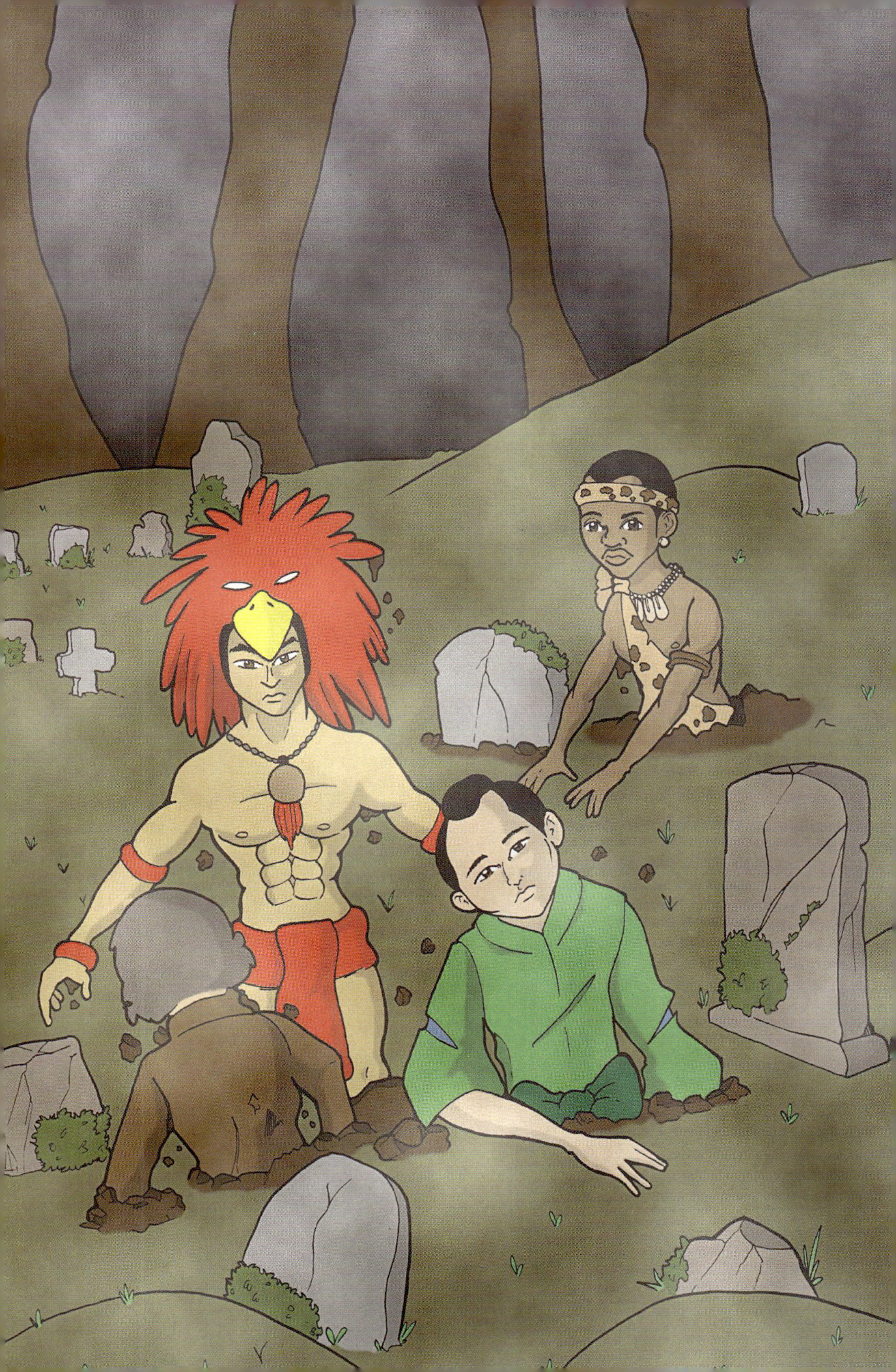

The children are without respect for their parents and the elders. We must go to look in on them. It is time to pay these young ones a visit. Come! We have slept long enough. Come, now, we must go!"

After hearing this news, the men prepared themselves to leave for city. They wanted to look in on their great-great-great-grandchildren and see them for the very first time. They were all excited!

When the Hunter and the men of old also known as the Ancient Ones, arrived in town, they saw many things that made them sad. The Ancient Ones didn't waste any time. They went straight to Grandfather's house. When Grandfather opened the door the same strong wind that he felt as he walked back down the mountain caught his attention. It was at that moment Grandfather knew the wind coming from around the Hunter's cape was the same brush of wind he felt the other day. Grandfather welcomed the men into his home. The men and Grandfather communed for a while, and during that time, Grandfather gave the Ancient Ones some unpleasant news. He explained to the Hunter, "Fatou is your great-great-great granddaughter, and she and I are worried about many of the Ancient Ones' great-great-great-grandchildren. They are joining clans which they now call gangs, and they doing all kinds of dishonorable things."

After hearing all the disturbing news, the Hunter and the Ancient Ones talked amongst themselves. The

Hunter then turned to his great grandson (Grandfather) and asked his permission to visit the homes of his neighborhood. Speaking with amazement, Grandfather replied, "Why do you ask permission from me, someone so weak beneath your greatness?" The Hunter smiled and replied, "You see, it doesn't matter how great or small someone is, what matters is the respect that is due when someone enters another's home or land. Just as you asked permission to enter our sacred burial ground, when you visited us that day, we must show you the same respect; for this neighborhood is your sacred ground." Grandfather respected the Hunter's request and granted him permission.

The Hunter and the Ancient Ones' plan was to visit the homes within the neighborhood and ask permission of the parents to take any troubled youth back with them, to their village for special character training. They promised to treat the children with care, but before they could leave Grandfather's house, word traveled quickly throughout the neighborhood, that the graves were opened. The traveling salesman had told everyone, that morning, what he had heard and saw when he had returned from the mountain. Then one neighbor after another heard the shocking news and ran to Grandfather's to let him know what happen. That's when the neighbors met the Hunter and the Ancient Ones. The neighbors had brought their children with them, and mothers and fathers were crying out, "Please take our sons and daughters! Help us save them from a life of destruction and the dangers that await them within our streets."

The Hunter and the Ancient Ones were moved with compassion and before long they had hundreds of children to care for. The need was too great for them to bear alone so they asked the neighbors to come with them to the mountaintop and help them train and care for the young. There was one more thing to do before they left the city.

The Hunter sent the Ancient Ones back to get Fatou so they could place her in the front of the line as a symbol of honor because everyone knew had it not been for Fatou, her grandfather would have never visited the graveyard to summon the men of old.

For so long, everyone was turning their heads and adapted to the immoralities that plagued their neighborhood. On their journey back to the village, there appeared the Warrior with two young men. The Warrior was a ferocious looking being that had a strong statue. Startled by the Warrior's presence, the Hunter questioned, "What business do you have with us on our journey to the mountaintop?"

The Warrior had done many hurtful things to mankind but now he wanted to help. He stepped onto the road and knelt down before the hunter. He bowed his head and asked the Hunter to forgive him for all the evil he caused throughout the land. The Warrior humbly stated, "You're Greatness, for generation to generation, I have spread my evil spirit among mankind. I have done so many evil things because of my jealousy to seek your place of greatness. I hated you because you were loved throughout the land and I coveted your position as number one so I set an eternal goal to destroy everything that you planned to make good. I destroyed your villages and innocent lives that I can never replace, but I do want to ask for your Greatness' forgiveness and offer my sincere assistance to make things right once more."

The Warrior continued to plead, "Your Greatness, I have committed a great injustice upon your villages and mankind. It is due to my selfish and jealous desires to be greater than you, and become the most powerful being, that I brought shame and dishonor to myself and this great land. And because of my wickedness, I have unleashed an evil spirit that has destroyed neighbors and their neighborhoods, as well as these two young men who robbed the bus driver and stole the children's joy." Hearing this plea from the once feared Warrior, the Hunter raised his hand and proclaimed, "Your wrong doings have been forgiven! Come join us on the mountaintop." Rising from his position of humbleness, the Warrior made a strong grunting sound and said to the two young men, "Come! Now!" The young men started to follow the

Warrior and then stopped. They turned to Fatou and the crowd and squeaked out, "Us, too? Can we be forgiven?"

Once more the Hunter was moved with compassion. He turned to Fatou and the crowd. He stated, "This is your day in time and only you can judge, convict, or forgive the wrong doings of this era. Even though we are all one, each generation has to be responsible and accountable for their actions in their lifetime. I have forgiven the Warrior but the rest is up to you."

Understanding the words of the Hunter, Fatou turned to her neighbors and proclaimed "I forgive these young men that robbed us of our joy and our right to live in peace." The neighbors looked at each other and one by one they proclaimed. "I forgive them. I forgive them..." After a while all the people had forgiven the young men and asked them to join the journey to the mountain top.

The Hunter, the Ancient Ones, the Warrior, the two young men, the neighbors, and the troubled youths finally reached the mountaintop. They entered the village and set up the camp for training, resting, and eating.

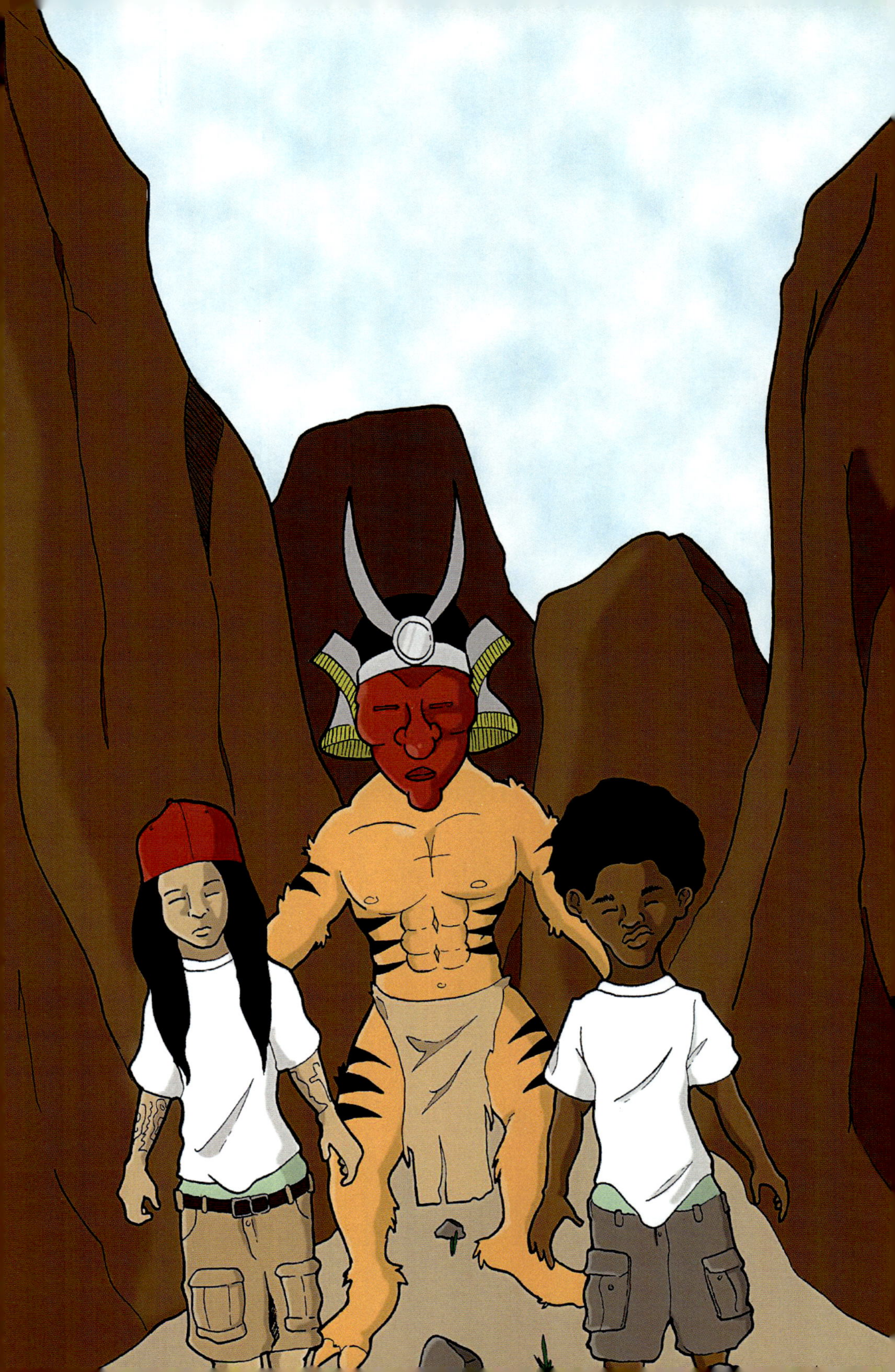

The training was very intense. The Ancient Ones and the neighbors that came to the mountaintop, kept the youth very busy. They taught them skills from long ago and showed them how to apply them for the skills needed in today's world. However, the Hunter and the Warrior taught the most important lesson of them all, which was living together in peace. The Hunter and the Warrior demonstrated that through love, compassion can be formed; from compassion, forgiveness can be rendered; and through forgiveness, harmony is present.

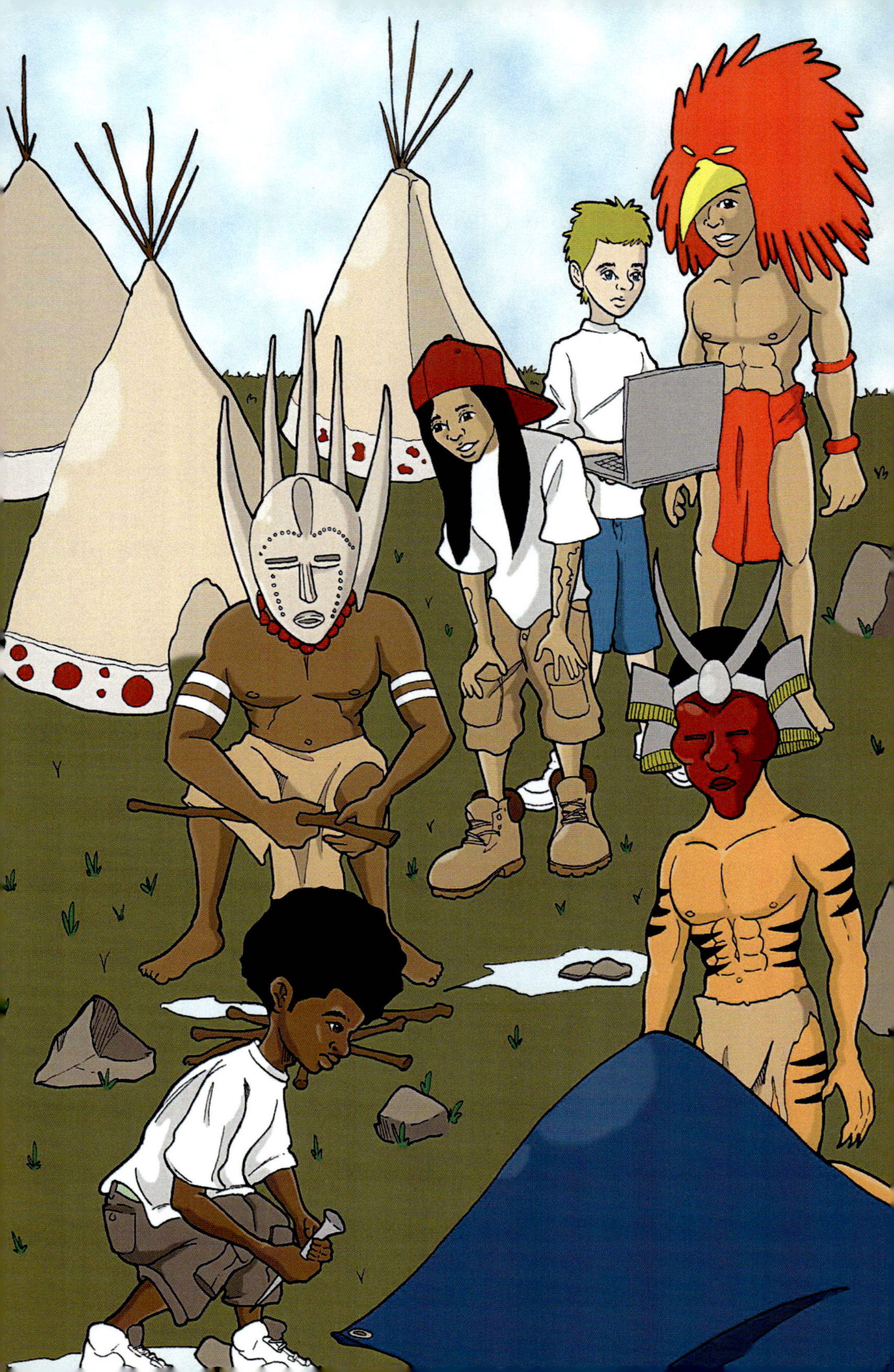

After several months of living on the mountaintop to receive moral building, good work ethics, and valuable skills, it was time for the two young men who had robbed Mr. Jayrel; and all the young people of the neighborhood, to return to their families and friends. They had been well trained with necessary skills needed for their journey through life.

At last, the time had come and a ceremony was held to honor the youth. The Ancient Ones gave them many gifts from the days of old. The young men and children kept these gifts as family treasures to be passed down through generations to come.

It was now time for all the hard work of the Ancient Ones and the Warrior to be put to the test.

The Hunter instructed all the youth to pass down the teachings which they had learned from the men of old, and most of all, the Hunter encouraged the young people to always try to demonstrate forgiveness whenever possible. It was now time for everybody to go back to their homes in the city.

The neighbors took down the camps to give the youth time to rest before their journey back down the mountain. During the time the neighbors had spent together on the mountaintop, they learned to trust each other. Grandfather and Fatou watched their friends as they walked down the mountain and back to their neighborhood.

Years later, the children that followed Fatou up

the mountain, to the ancient graveyard were now adults. The children had grown older and they told their sons and daughters about the Hunter and the Ancient Ones. They told their story over and over again. They told the story for years and years and for generation to generation. They boasted how they owed everything to Fatou, and that nothing would have ever changed without Fatou taking a stand against the once, evil Warrior's spirit, that had spread over their neighborhood as a blanket covers a bed.

The young men that had been forgiven for their wrong, were much older, too, and lived in the neighborhood which they once brought sadness. The neighbors gave testimonies, "If it had not been for the

Hunter, the Ancient Ones, and the Warrior, working together, we would not have ever learned the skills that turned our lives around, in order to teach our children in the right way." But most of all, the young men spoke to their children and neighbors about the most valuable lessons of all, peace. They gratefully commented, "We learned how to live in peace and harmony through love and compassion." And because of the life changing testimonies, Fatou became the most honored person in her neighborhood, just as the Hunter was long ago. Fatou was so admired that many young girls in the neighborhood wanted to be a "life changer" like her.

The traveling salesman, who was the first to see

the ancient village, moved back into neighborhood and opened a business where he employed several children from the neighborhood. He told his story over and over again of how he could not sleep the night the Hunter and the Ancient Ones came into town because he heard voices talking throughout the night, on the mountaintop. He said, "I did not know where the voices were coming from, and I didn't know it was the Hunter and the Ancient Ones talking among them." The salesman continued, "What was even more amazing and bizarre was that everyone said no flowers were present when the neighbors went down the mountain from the training camp. But on the one year anniversary of the Hunter's visit to our neighborhood the town's people revisited the training grounds and to everyone's amazement, beautiful flowers had grown up and covered the old burial ground as if it was a floral shop."

He continued, "The beautiful picture of that graveyard will always be etched in my mind. It is so vivid I can still see those beautiful flowers of all colors. And most of all, I love to tell the story of love, forgiveness, and peace I felt after that day ... that is the reason why I chose to come back to this neighborhood to live the rest of my days out and to help reach out to the youth in the neighborhood because of the lessons I learned from Fatou's courageous act to restore the neighborhood back to love, hope, and peace.

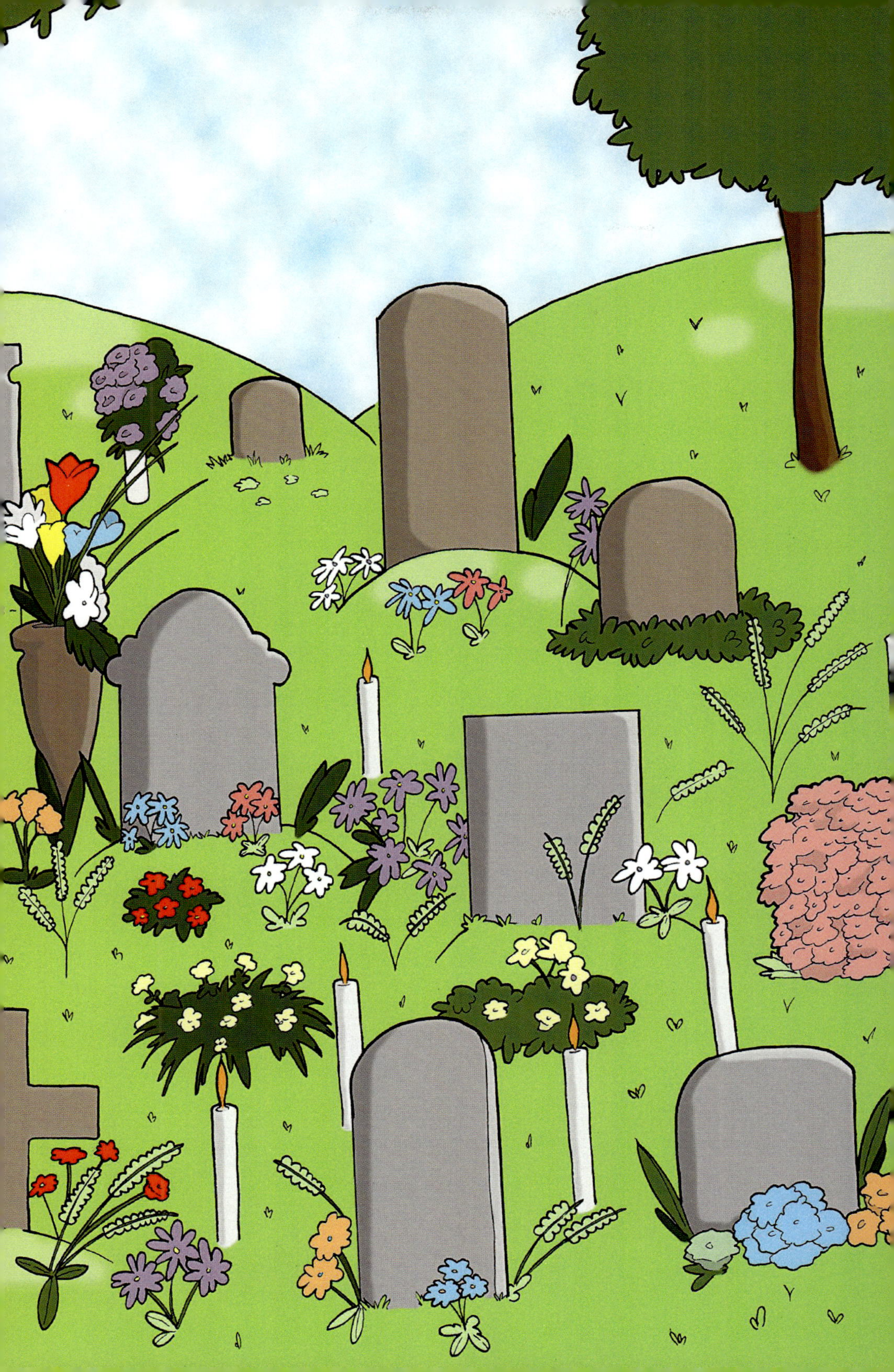

Not to mention all the positive lessons I was taught from the Manuel, *The Good Neighbor.* And the lessons I learned by watching the Hunter and the Warrior working side by side for the good of the neighborhood, that was an awesome day I will remember."

Fatou, now older, still remembers the Hunter and the Ancient Ones visit to the neighborhood as if it was yesterday. And whenever Fatou was asked, which is often, about that great day, she takes the time to share her story about the Hunter and the Ancient Ones. Instead of a wooden box in front of her yard, Fatou now makes her seat in the middle of the public square where she tells her story of the Hunter and the Ancient

Ones visit to her home, and how much she misses her grandfather's wisdom. Fatou tells how the flowers mysteriously appeared, in the sacred burial ground and covered the ancient graves. She also told how no one in the neighborhood believed that anything beautiful would ever grow in that old graveyard, and how the neighbors felt nothing good would ever happen for their neighborhood until the Hunter and the Ancient Ones came and gave them hope. Fatou goes on to tell how the traveler came into the town and told what he saw, and on that great day, how quickly his words traveled throughout the neighborhood.

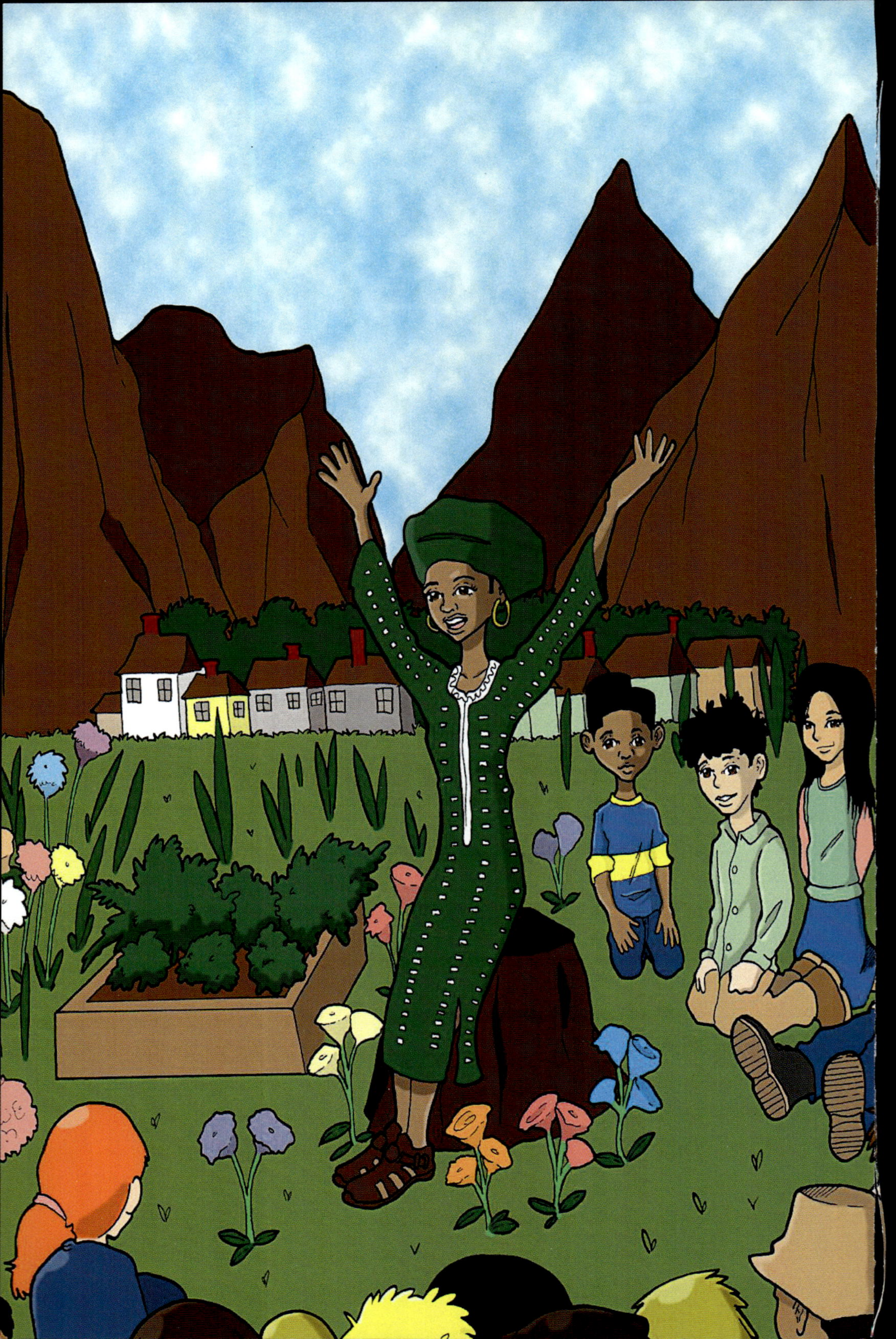

Fatou continues, "Mothers and fathers were crying with exceeding joy because they began to believe that something good could possibly happen for our neighborhood and for the children of the neighborhood." Fatou tells how she remembers Grandfather taking Mr. Jayrel to the mountaintop to show him the miracle in the old burial ground and he had no more fear of the neighborhood. Fatou talked about the restoring of the annual trips to the zoo that still continues, today. Yes, the great pursuit to the mountaintop worked! The neighborhood was once again safe to live in; for the old and the young were working together in peace, love, and harmony. And in honor and memory of Fatou's grandfather and the anniversary of the Hunter and the Ancient Ones' visit to their neighborhood, Fatou and the neighbors will visit the burial ground with beautiful flowers and gifts. Then a small child from each household in the neighborhood will walk over to the ancestors' resting place and present a token of honor and appreciation for paving the way many years ago. The children will then give their reports, to the men of old (the Hunter and the Ancient Ones), about the neighborhood and what each child is doing to uphold the Manuel, *The Good Neighbor*. Then each child will present their token of love and appreciation to their ancestors and say, "All is well in the neighborhood, so rest in peace..., men of old."

THE HUNTER
THE GREAT ONE

THE WARRIOR
THE BRAVE ONE

THE ANCIENT
WISDOM

THE ANCIENT
PRIDE

THE ANCIENT
HOPE

One year after leaving the graveyard ceremony, Fatou noticed something that she had not seen since she was a young girl, and only once on the day the young men and children had finished their training...butterflies!

For years, the butterflies had left Fatou's neighborhood because of all the ugliness of evil that hovered over the town. However, the butterflies only came back because of the continuous beauty of love, peace, and harmony which now dwells in the township where Fatou and her neighbors still live. It was a beautiful sight to the neighborhood children who only dreamed of seeing the butterflies that they had often heard their parents talk about.

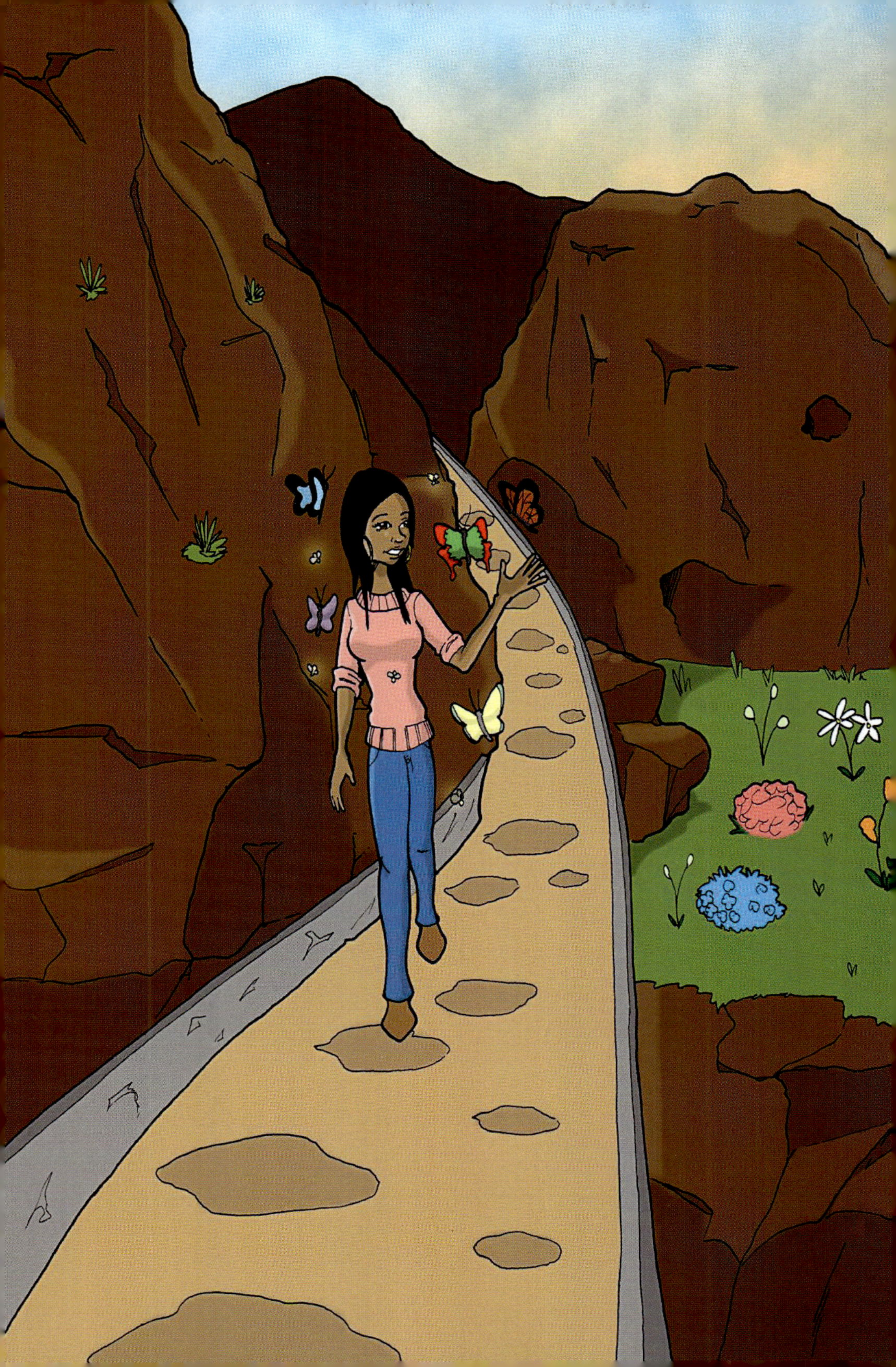

Fatou remembered those very dark days in her neighborhood. Nevertheless, to Fatou, this time it was different. The butterflies had just appeared and were following her back down the mountain. This was a beautiful sight to Fatou as she wondered what was going on. Suddenly the same wind that she remembered her grandfather said he felt was what Fatou felt, but not quite as strong. But just as it came, it went away. The wind had gently blown the butterflies into the neighborhood. They were everywhere. The butterflies started dancing in the air as if they were celebrating the lasting peace that had fallen over the neighborhood since the Hunter and the Ancient Ones went back to their resting place on top of the mountain.

Fatou knew her work was done well, and restoring her neighborhood was her purpose as a child; to lead the great pursuit of love, peace, and harmony. From one little girl's unselfish act and her desire to live in peace and harmony, within her neighborhood, Fatou brought a positive change in the lives of others. She had joined people from every age, race, and cultural diversity to help restore a dying neighborhood. Yes, one little girl that saw her neighborhood as a whole unit, and as her family, brought what others saw as just a dream to reality.

One day as the sun was going down the lightning bugs appeared so bright that they lit the streets of the neighborhood. Fatou smiled and as she settled in for the night. She gave thanks to her grandparents and parents for teaching her the right way to live in harmony with others. She also gave thanks to them for teaching her morals and principles, as well as giving her guidelines to live by such as the Manuel, *The Good Neighbor*. She also gave thanks to all the ancestors for starting the never ending path of life -- for all humanity.

There was not a day or night that Fatou did not think on those moments and about what her family and the men of old taught her. And every night that Fatou fell asleep, little did she know that the ancient village would appear on the mountaintop above the ancestral graves and would continue to do so for generations to come ....